THE 28 MANSIONS OF THE MOON
(Lunar Mansions)

Written by Alana Ennis

WHAT IS A LUNAR MANSION?

Arabic astrology has long spoken of the mansions of the moon. There are 28 mansions, divided by 360 degrees, each mansion holds a space in the sky of approximately 12.85 degrees, 51 minutes, 26 seconds of arc. They are positioned (boundaried) in a specific constellation (group of stars) of the zodiac (e.g. Aries, Taurus, Gemini etc). Because of this, each mansion is responsible for an approximate 13-day period each year.

To further complicate this, the mansions will also be present at least once each month, this is due to the moons complete monthly cycle through the zodiac (see my other book "The Moon" for more information on this).

This book will explain all 28 mansions to you, the dates they rule (both ancient Islamic, and modern), their ruling planets, ruling sign(s)/constellations (both ancient Islamic, and modern), their nature, and their significance.

You can find the current mansion position each month by knowing where the moon is located at any given time. E.g. If the moon is located at 08 LEO 33' 11", then the moon is in the 10th Mansion. Furthermore, if you need to know the mansion position for any specific week, you can search the date in this book, and it will tell you the mansion. E.g., 25th December is the 21st Mansion (according to the ancient Islamic astrology system), and 19th Mansion according to modern astrology.

You can find the current moon position in any good Astrology program, or Google (of course!).

AUTHOR NOTES

The mansions can become complex, due to many historical manuscripts and books with competing ideas. The dates provided in this book for each mansion are for reference only, the only true way to calculate the mansion is to know exactly where the moon is located on any given day.

However, I prefer the ancient Islamic astrology system for calculating the mansions annual dates and positions. It is my default method.

Keep in mind the 1st mansion always starts at 00 ARIES 00' 00" (sometimes astrologers would place the 28th mansion, "The Belly of the Fish", in this 1st position).

At the end of this book, I have included the Gregorian mansion dates, as found on Wikipedia. And Athanasius Kircher' version of the mansions, which shows the 28th Mansion "The Belly of the Fish" in the 1st mansion position.

I cannot cover ALL variations of the mansions in this book. Instead, the reader should choose whatever method works best for them.

The 28 Mansions of the Moon

1st Lunar Mansion: The Two Signs, The Final Generation, Horns of Aries, Ram's Horns, The Horns.

Position: This Mansion starts from 00 ARIES 00' 00" and ends at 12 ARIES 51' 22".

Annual Dates: 5th April to 17th April (Ancient), 23rd April to 10th May (Current).

Ruling Constellation: The constellation originally associated with this mansion is **Aries**. The principal stars associated with this mansion are Sheratan (beta Aries) and Mesarthim (gamma Aries). The current constellation is **Taurus**.

Planets: Mars and Sun.

Attribute: The First Intellect, the Pen.

Divine Attribute: Divine Essence.

Significance: Journeys and discord.

Good for taking medicines, pasturing livestock, making journey, except second hour.

Good for buying tame animals, for journeys, especially voyages, for making arms, planting trees, cutting hair or nails, putting on new clothes.

Bad for contracting marriage (holds for Moon in Aries), making partnerships, or buying slaves, who will be bad, disobedient, or run away. If captured, prison will be bad and strong.

2nd Lunar Mansion: The Ram's Belly, The Belly of Aries, The Belly of the Ram, The Belly of Aries.

Position: This Mansion starts from 12 ARIES 51' 22" and ends at 25 ARIES 42' 51".

Annual Dates: 18th April to 30th April (Ancient), 11th May to 19th May (Current).

Ruling Constellation: The constellation originally associated with this mansion is **Aries**. The principal star associated with this mansion is Botein (delta Aries). The current constellation is **Taurus**.

Planets: Mars and Moon.

Attribute: The Universal Soul, The Preserved Tablet, The Guarded Table.

Divine Attribute: The One Who Calls Forth, He Who Invokes.

Significance: Finding treasure and retaining captives.

Good for sowing and making journeys.

Bad for marriage, buying slaves, and for boats and prisoners.

3rd Lunar Mansion: The Many Little Ones, Hen of the Skies with her Children, Rainy Ones, The Pleiades, The Seven Sisters.

Position: This Mansion starts from 25 ARIES 42' 51" and ends at 08 TAURUS 34' 17".

Annual Dates: 1st May to 13th May (Ancient), 20th May to 29th May (Current).

Ruling Constellation: The constellation originally associated with this mansion is **Taurus**. The principal star associated with this mansion is Alcyone (eta Taurus). The current constellation is **Gemini**.

Planets: Venus and Mars.

Attribute: The Universal Nature.

Divine Attribute: The Interior.

Significance: Profits sailors, huntsmen, alchemists.

Good for trading and revenge on enemies; indifferent for travel.

Good for buying tame animals and hunting, for all matters involving fire, and for doing good.

Bad for marriage, and making partnerships, especially with those more powerful. Bad for buying cattle or flocks, for planting trees, sowing, or putting on new clothes. If captured, prison will be strong and long.

Water journeys will bring fear and danger.

4th Lunar Mansion: The Follower, Bull's Eye, Eye or Head of Taurus.

Position: This Mansion starts from 08 TAURUS 34' 17" and ends at 21 TAURUS 25' 40".

Annual Dates: 14th May to 26th May (Ancient), 30th May to 13th June (Current).

Ruling Constellation: The constellation originally associated with this mansion is **Taurus**. The principal star associated with this mansion is Aldebaran (alpha Taurus). The current constellation is **Gemini**.

Planets: Venus and Mercury.

Attribute: Universal Substance, Prima Materia.

Divine Attribute: The Last.

Significance: Destruction and hinderances of buildings, fountains, wells and gold mines, the flight of reptiles and creates discord.

Good for sowing, for putting on new clothes, for receiving women and feminine things, for demolishing a building or starting a new one, for making a journey, except for third part of day.

Good to build a house, which will be solid, and building in general, to dig a ditch, to buy slaves, who will be loyal and honest, and to buy livestock. Also, good to be with kings and lords, for receiving power or honours.

Bad to contract marriage, since woman will prefer another, or to enter partnerships, especially with those more powerful. Voyages will involve big waves. If captured, the captivity will be long but, if captured for skills, will be released through goodwill.

5th Lunar Mansion: A White Spot, The Hunter's Head.

Position: This Mansion starts from 21 TAURUS 25' 40" and ends at 04 GEMINI 17' 09".

Annual Dates: 27th May to 8th June (Ancient), 14th June to 29th June (Current).

Ruling Constellation: The constellation originally associated with this mansion is **Orion**. The principal star associated with this mansion is Meissa (lambda Orion). The current constellation is **Gemini/Cancer**.

Planets: Mercury and Jupiter.

Attribute: Universal Body.

Divine Attribute: The Manifest.

Significance: Helps safe return from journey, instruction of pupils, confirms buildings, gives health and good will.

Good for contracting marriage, for putting boys to study laws, scriptures or writing, for making medicines, for making a journey.

Good for buying slaves, who will be good and loyal, for building, for travel by water, for washing head, indeed general washing, and cutting hair.

Bad for partnerships. If captured, imprisonment will be long, unless captured for skills, when he will escape.

6th Lunar Mansion: A Brand or Mark, The Mark, Mark on Foot (of Pollux), Little Star of Great Light.

Position: This Mansion starts from 04 GEMINI 17' 09" and ends at 17 GEMINI 08' 34".

Annual Dates: 9th June to 21st June (Ancient), 30th June to 11th July (Current).

Ruling Constellation: The constellation originally associated with this mansion is **Gemini**. The principal star associated with this mansion is Alhena (gamma Gemini). The current constellation is **Cancer**.

Planets: Mercury and Venus.

Attribute: Form.

Divine Attribute: The Wise.

Significance: Favours hunting, besieging towns, revenge of princes, destroys harvests and fruits, hinders medicine.

Good for kings to declare war, enrolment of armies and cavalry, for knights seeking better pay, for the successful siege of a city, for smiting enemies and evildoers.

Good for partnerships and ventures, associates will agree and be honest and loyal, for hunting, for journeys by water, though delays.

Bad for taking medicine and for treating wounds. New clothes put on will soon tear. If captured, release within three days or very long imprisonment. Bad for sowing, seeking a loan, or burial.

7th Lunar Mansion: The Forearm, Arm of Gemini.

Position: This Mansion starts from 17 GEMINI 08' 34" and ends at 00 CANCER 00' 00".

Annual Dates: 22nd June to 4th July (Ancient), 12th July to 29th July (Current).

Ruling Constellation: The constellation originally associated with this mansion is **Gemini**. The principal stars associated with this mansion are Castor (alpha Gemini) and Pollux (beta Gemini). The current constellation is **Cancer/Leo**.

Planets: Mercury and Saturn.

Attribute: The Throne.

Divine Attribute: The All-Encompassing.

Significance: Brings money and friendship, profits lovers, disperses flies, destroys teaching authorities.

Good for ploughing and sowing, for putting on new clothes, for women's jewellery, for cavalry.

Good for partnerships, which will be good and useful, with loyal and agreeable associates, for washing head, cutting hair and new clothes, for buying slaves and livestock, for smiting or making peace with enemies, for voyages towards destination, but delays on return.

Bad for journeys, except in last third of night. Bad for buying land, and for giving up medicine. If captured, unless he escapes in three days, he will die in prison. Likewise, if he has escaped something he fears, he will encounter it again.

8th Lunar Mansion: Misty or Cloudy, The Gap or Crib.

Position: This Mansion starts from 00 CANCER 00' 00" and ends at 12 CANCER 51' 22".

Annual Dates: 5th July to 17th July (Ancient), 30th July to 9th August (Current).

Ruling Constellation: The constellation originally associated with this mansion is **Cancer**. The principal star associated with this mansion is Praesaepe (M44 Cancer). The current constellation is **Leo**.

Planets: Moon and Sun.

Attribute: The Footstool.

Divine Attribute: The Grateful.

Significance: Creates, love, friendship, travellers' fellowship, drives away mice, confirms captivity.

Good for taking medicine, for cutting new clothes, for women's jewellery and putting it on. Rain will bring benefit not damage.

Good for voyages, swift on outward and return journeys. Marriages contracted will be harmonious for a while, then discordant.

Bad for travel, except for last third of night. A slave bought will be deceitful, accuse his master, and run away. A partnership started will involve fraud on either side. If captured, long imprisonment.

9th Lunar Mansion: Lion's Eye, The Glance, The Glance of the Lion's Eye, Eye of Leo.

Position: This Mansion starts from 12 CANCER 51' 22" and ends at 25 CANCER 42' 51".

Annual Dates: 18th July to 30th July (Ancient), 10th August to 19th August (Current).

Ruling Constellation: The constellation originally associated with this mansion is **Leo**. The principal star associated with this mansion is Alterf (lambda Leo). The current constellation is **Leo**.

Planets: Sun and Moon.

Attribute: The Self-Existing Ultimate Sphere, the Starless Sky, the Zodiacal Towers.

Divine Attribute: The Independent, the Rich.

Significance: Hinders harvests and travellers, creates discord between men.

Good for voyages, outward and return, for reinforcing doors and making locks, for making beds and putting up bed-curtains, for transplanting wheat.

Bad for sowing, journeys, entrusting anything to anyone, or seeking to harm anyone. Bad for partnerships, which will involve fraud on either side. Bad for cutting hair, or new clothes. Putting on new clothes may lead to drowning in them. If captured, long imprisonment.

10th Lunar Mansion: Lion's Forehead, The Forehead, Neck or Forehead of Leo.

Position: This Mansion starts from 25 CANCER 42' 51" and ends at 08 LEO 34' 17".

Annual Dates: 31st July to 13th August (Ancient), 20th August to 2nd September (Current).

Ruling Constellation: The constellation originally associated with this mansion is **Leo**. The principal stars associated with this mansion are Regulus (alpha Leo), Algieba (gamma Leo), Adhafera (zeta Leo), and Al Jabhah (eta Leo). The current constellation is **Leo/Virgo**.

Planets: Sun and Mars.

Attribute: The Sky of the Fixed Stars, the Sphere of the Stations, the Sun of Paradise, the Roof of Hell.

Divine Attribute: The Powerful.

Significance: Strengthens buildings, extends love, good will and help against enemies.

Good for contracting marriage, for sugar and what is made with it.

Good for buildings, which will last, and for partnerships, benefiting all parties. If captured, at the command of a leader or because of great deed, and long, hard imprisonment.

Bad for journeys and entrusting anything, for putting on new clothes or for women's jewellery.

11th Lunar Mansion: Lion's Mane, The Mane, Leo's Mane.

Position: This Mansion starts from 08 LEO 34' 17" and ends at 21 LEO 25' 40".

Annual Dates: 14th August to 26th August (Ancient), 3rd September to 13th September (Current).

Ruling Constellation: The constellation originally associated with this mansion is **Leo.** The principal stars originally associated with this mansion are Zosma (delta Leo) and Coxa (theta Leo). The current constellation is **Virgo.**

Planets: Sun and Mercury.

Attribute: The First Heaven, the Sphere of Saturn, the Sky of the Visited House and Lotus of the Extreme.

Divine Attribute: The Lord.

Significance: Helps journeys and money from commerce, and redeeming captives.

Good for sowing and planting, for besieging. Indifferent for trade and journeys.

Good for buildings and foundations, which will last, and for partnerships, from which associates will gain. Good for cutting hair.

Bad for freeing captives. Bad for new clothes. If captured, at the command of a leader, and long imprisonment.

12th Lunar Mansion: Lion's Tail, The Changer, Tail of Leo.

Position: This Mansion starts from 21 LEO 25' 40" and ends at 04 VIRGO 17' 09".

Annual Dates: 27th August to 8th September (Ancient), 14th September to 19th September (Current).

Ruling Constellation: The constellation originally associated with this mansion is **Leo**. The principal star associated with this mansion is Denebola (beta Leo). The current constellation is **Virgo**.

Planets: Sun and Jupiter.

Attribute: The Second Heaven, the Sphere of Jupiter, the Abode of Musa (Moses).

Divine Attribute: The Knowing.

Significance: Prospers harvests and plantations, betters' servants, captives, and allies, but hinders sailors.

Good for starting all building, for arranging lands, sowing, and planting, for marriage, for putting on new clothes, for women's jewellery, for making a journey in the first third of day.

Good for buying slaves and livestock, once the Moon is out of Leo, since the Lion is the great devourer. (If he eats a lot it leads to stomach pains, power, boldness, and obstinacy.)

What is lent will not be returned, or only with great effort and delay. Voyages will be long, hard, and dangerous, but not fatal.

13th Lunar Mansion: Dogs, Winged Ones of Virgo, The Barker, Sirius,

Position: This Mansion starts from 04 VIRGO 17' 09" and ends at 17 VIRGO 08' 34".

Annual Dates: 9th September to 21st September (Ancient), 20th September to 15th October (Current).

Ruling Constellation: The constellation originally associated with this mansion is **Virgo**. The principal stars associated with this mansion are Zavijava (beta Virgo), Zaniah (eta Virgo), Porrima (gamma Virgo), Auva (delta Virgo), and Vindemiatrix (epsilon Virgo). The current constellation is **Virgo/Libra**.

Planets: Mercury and Venus.

Attribute: The Third Heaven, the Sphere of Mars, the Abode of Harun (Aaron).

Divine Attribute: The Victorious.

Significance: Favours benevolence, money, voyages, harvests, freedom of captives.

Good to plough, sow, make a journey, marry, free captives.

Good to buy a slave, who will be good, loyal, and honest, to start building, to give oneself to pleasures and jokes, to come before a king or famous man, to take medicines, to cut new clothes, to wash or cut hair.

Not bad to marry a corrupted woman, and, if marrying a virgin, the marriage will last a while.

A voyage undertaken will involve delay in return. If captured, he will be injured in prison, but captivity will end well.

14th Lunar Mansion: Ear of Wheat, The Unarmed, Virgo's Ear of Corn.

Position: This Mansion starts from 17 VIRGO 08' 34" and ends at 00 LIBRA 00' 00".

Annual Dates: 22nd September to 4th October (Ancient), 16th October to 25th October (Current).

Ruling Constellation: The constellation originally associated with this mansion is **Virgo**. The principal star associated with this mansion is Spica (alpha Virgo). The current constellation is **Libra/Scorpio**.

Planets: Mercury and Saturn.

Attribute: The Forth Heaven, the Sphere of the Sun, the Abode of Idris (Enoch, Hermes).

Divine Attribute: The Light.

Significance: Favours marital love, healing of sick, good for journeys by sea but bad for land.

Good for marrying a woman who is not a virgin, for medicines, sowing and planting.

Good to start a voyage and a partnership, which will be profitable and harmonious, to buy a slave, who will be good, honest, and respectful.

Marriage with a virgin will not last long, and it is not bad to marry a corrupted woman. If captured, he will soon escape or be released.

15th Lunar Mansion: Covered or Flying Covered, The Covering, The Cover, The Veil.

Position: This Mansion starts from 00 LIBRA 00' 00" and ends at 12 LIBRA 51' 22".

Annual Dates: 5th October to 17th October (Ancient), 26th October to 6th November (Current).

Ruling Constellation: The constellation originally associated with this mansion is **Virgo**. The principal star associated with this mansion is Syrma (iota Virgo). The current constellation is **Scorpio**.

Planets: Mercury and Sun.

Attribute: The Fifth Heaven, the Sphere of Venus, the Abode of Yusuf (Joseph).

Divine Attribute: The Form-Giver.

Significance: Good for extracting treasures, digging pits, helps divorce, discord, destruction of houses and enemies, hinders travel.

Good to dig wells and ditches, to cure illnesses to do with wind, but not others.

Good for moving house, for adapting or preparing a house, its owner and site. Good to seek to do a good deed, to buy and sell, but selling slaves not livestock.

Bad for journeys. Bad for both land and sea journeys. Marriage will not last in harmony, or only for a while. Partnerships entered will lead to fraud and discord. Money lent will not be returned. Bad for cutting hair.

16th Lunar Mansion: Scorpion's Claw, The Claws, Horns of Scorpio.

Position: This Mansion starts from 12 LIBRA 51' 22" and ends at 25 LIBRA 42' 51".

Dates: 18th October to 30th October (Ancient), 7th November to 23rd November (Current).

Ruling Constellation: The constellation originally associated with this mansion is **Libra**. The principal stars associated with this mansion are Zuben Elgenubi(alpha Libra) and Zuben Eschemali (beta Libra). The current constellation is **Scorpio/Sagittarius**.

Planets: Venus and Moon.

Attribute: The Sixth Heaven, the Sphere of Mercury, the Abode of 'Isa (Jesus).

Divine Attribute: The Numberer.

Significance: Hinders journeys and marriage, harvests, and commerce, but helps redemption of captives.

A slave bought will be good, loyal, and honest.

Bad for marriage, which will only last in harmony for a while, for partnerships, which will lead to dishonesty and mutual suspicion. Bad for journeys, trade, medicines, sowing, women's jewellery, for cutting or putting on new clothes. If captured, he will soon be out of prison, if God wills.

17th Lunar Mansion: Scorpion's Crown, The Crown of the Forehead, Crown of Scorpio.

Position: This Mansion starts from 25 LIBRA 42' 51" and ends at 08 SCORPIO 34' 17".

Dates: 31st October to 12th November (Ancient), 24th November to 30th November (Current).

Ruling Constellation: The constellation originally associated with this mansion is **Scorpius**. The principal stars associated with this mansion are Graffias or Acrab (beta Scorpius) and Dschubba (delta Scorpius). The current constellation is **Sagittarius**.

Planets: Pluto and Mars.

Attribute: The Seventh Heaven, the Sphere of the Moon, the Abode of Adam.

Divine Attribute: The Evident.

Significance: Improves bad fortune, helps love to last, strengthens buildings, helps sailors.

Good to buy flocks and livestock, to change their pasture, to put on new jewellery and besiege towns.

Good for starting building, which will be solid and durable, for settling a dispute between two people, to foster love, and love begun will be absolutely solid and last forever. Good for all medicine.

Voyages started will bring anxiety and sorrows, but he will survive. Partnerships started will bring discord, and he who marries, will find his wife impure. Bad for selling slaves or cutting hair.

18th Lunar Mansion: Scorpion's Heart, The Heart, Heart of Scorpio.

Position: This Mansion starts from 08 SCORPIO 34' 17" and ends at 21 SCORPIO 25' 40".

Dates: 13th November to 25th November (Ancient), 1st December to 14th December (Current).

Ruling Constellation: The constellation originally associated with this mansion is **Scorpius**. The principal star associated with this mansion is Antares (alpha Scorpius). The current constellation is **Sagittarius**.

Planets: Pluto and Mercury.

Attribute: The Sphere of Ether, Meteors and Fire.

Divine Attribute: The Seizer.

Significance: Causes discord, sedition, conspiracy against powerful, revenge from enemies, but frees captives and helps buildings.

Good for building, for arranging lands and buying them, for receiving honours and power. If it begins to rain, it will be wholesome, useful, and good. Eastwards journeys are favoured.

Building undertaken will be solid. Good for planting and taking medicines. If a man gets married and the Mars is with the Moon here, he will find her not to be a virgin. If he enters a ship, he will come out again.

Bad for selling slaves, new clothes, cutting hair. Partnerships will result in discord.

19th Lunar Mansion: Scorpion's Sting, The Mansion of Chastity, The Sting, Tail of Scorpio.

Position: This Mansion starts from 21 SCORPIO 25' 40" and ends at 04 SAGITTARIUS 17' 09".

Dates: 26th November to 8th December (Ancient), 15th December to 31st December (Current).

Ruling Constellation: The constellation originally associated with this mansion is **Scorpius**. The principal stars associated with this mansion are Shaula (lambda Scorpius) and Lesath (upsilon Scorpius). The current constellation is **Sagittarius/Capricorn**.

Planets: Pluto and Jupiter.

Attribute: Air.

Divine Attribute: The Living One.

Significance: Helps besieging and taking of cities, driving people from positions, destroys sailors and captives.

Good for besieging towns and encampments, for disputing against enemies, for making a journey, for sowing and for planting trees.

If a man gets married, he will find her not to be a virgin.

Bad for entrusting something to somebody. Bad for voyages, which will end in shipwreck, for partnerships, which will be discordant, for selling slaves, and very bad for a captive.

20th Lunar Mansion: Archer's Armpit, The Ostriches, Mansion of Delight and Favour (Influence), The Beam, Transom.

Position: This Mansion starts from 04 SAGITTARIUS 17' 09" and ends at 17 SAGITTARIUS 08' 34".

Dates: 9th December to 21st December (Ancient), 1st January to 6th January (Current).

Ruling Constellation: The constellation originally associated with this mansion is **Sagittarius**. The principal stars associated with this mansion are Ascella (zeta Sagittarius) and Nunki (sigma Sagittarius). The current constellation is **Capricorn**.

Planets: Jupiter and Venus.

Attribute: Water.

Divine Attribute: The Life-Giver.

Significance: Good for buying animals. Good for buying small animals. Rain will be good and do no harm. Indifferent for journeys.

Bad for partnerships and captivity.

21st Lunar Mansion: Archer's Head, The City, The Desert.

Position: This Mansion starts from 17 SAGITTARIUS 08' 34" and ends at 00 CAPRICORN 00' 00".

Dates: 22nd December to 3rd January (Ancient), 7th January to 23rd January (Current).

Ruling Constellation: The constellation originally associated with this mansion is **Sagittarius**. The principal star associated with this mansion is Albadah (pi Sagittarius). The current constellation is **Capricorn/Aquarius**.

Planets: Jupiter and Saturn.

Attribute: Earth.

Divine Attribute: The Death-Giver.

Significance: Favours harvests, money, buildings, travellers, causes divorce.

Good for starting any building, for sowing, for buying lands or livestock, for buying and making women's jewellery and clothes. Indifferent for journeys.

A woman who is divorced or widowed will not marry again. Indifferent for slaves bought, since they will think much of themselves and will not humble themselves to their masters.

22nd Lunar Mansion: Goat's Horn, The Arms of Sacrifice, The Lucky One of the Slaughterers, The Fortune of the Slayers, The Shepherd.

Position: This Mansion starts from 00 CAPRICORN 00' 00" and ends at 12 CAPRICORN 51' 22".

Dates: 4th January to 16th January (Ancient), 24th January to 1st February (Current).

Ruling Constellation: The constellation originally associated with this mansion is **Capricornus**. The principal stars associated with this mansion are Giedi Prima (alpha Capricornus) and Dabih (beta Capricornus). The current constellation is **Aquarius**.

Planets: Saturn and Sun.

Attribute: Minerals and Metals.

Divine Attribute: The Precious.

Significance: Incites the flight of slaves and captives, helping escape, and curing of diseases.

Good for medicine and journeys, except for last third of day. Good for putting on new clothes.

Good for entering a partnership, which will bring profit and usefulness, and for entering a ship, though there will be great anxieties from a strong desire to return and the like.

A man who becomes engaged will break the engagement before the wedding and die within six months, or the couple will be in conflict and live badly, with the wife mistreating the husband.

Bad for buying slaves, who will do ill to their master, or run away, or be irksome or bad. If captured, he will soon gain freedom.

23rd Lunar Mansion: Goat's Body, The Fortune of the Swallower, Swallowing.

Position: This Mansion starts from 12 CAPRICORN 51' 22" and ends at 25 CAPRICORN 42' 51".

Dates: 17th January to 29th January (Ancient), 2nd February to 11th February (Current).

Ruling Constellation: The constellation originally associated with this mansion is **Capricornus**. There is no principal star associated with this mansion. The current constellation is **Aquarius**.

Planets: Saturn and Moon.

Attribute: Plants.

Divine Attribute: The Nourisher.

Significance: Causes divorce, freedom of captives, healing of sick.

Good for partnerships. Good for medicine, for putting on new jewellery and clothes, for a journey in the middle third of day.

Bad to entrust something to someone. Bad for marriage, since wife will mistreat husband and they will not be together much, for entering a ship, if a short voyage is wanted, for buying slaves. If captured, he will soon regain liberty.

24th Lunar Mansion: Luckiest of the Lucky, The Fortune of the Fortunate, Star of Fortune.

Position: This Mansion starts from 25 CAPRICORN 42' 51" and ends at 08 AQUARIUS 34' 17".

Dates: 30th January to 11th February (Ancient), 12th February to 24th February (Current).

Ruling Constellation: The constellation originally associated with this mansion is **Aquarius**. The principal star associated with this mansion is Sadalsuud (beta Aquarius). The current constellation is **Aquarius/Pisces**.

Planets: Uranus and Mars.

Attribute: Animals.

Divine Attribute: The Humbler.

Significance: Helps marital understanding, victory of soldiers, causes disobedience, hindering execution of authority.

Good for medicine, sending out armies and soldiers. A slave bought will be strong, loyal, and good. Indifferent for journeys.

Bad for merchandise, jewellery, putting on new clothes, marrying. Bad for partnerships, which will end in great harm and conflict, and for entering a ship. Marriage will only last a while. If captured, he will soon be free.

25th Lunar Mansion: Lucky One of the King, The Fortune of the Hidden, Hiding Places, The Lucky Star of Hidden Things, The Butterfly Unfolding.

Position: This Mansion starts from 08 AQUARIUS 34' 17" and ends at 21 AQUARIUS 25' 40".

Dates: 12th February to 24th February (Ancient), 25th February to 12th March (Current).

Ruling Constellation: The constellation originally associated with this mansion is **Aquarius**. The principal stars associated with this mansion are Sadalbachia (gamma Aquarius) and Sadalmelik (alpha Aquarius). The current constellation is **Pisces**.

Planets: Uranus and Mercury.

Attribute: The Angels.

Divine Attribute: The Strong.

Significance: Helps siege and revenge, divorce, prisons and buildings, speeds messengers, destroys enemies, helps spells against sex or to cause impotence.

Good for besieging towns and encampments, for going into a quarrel, for pursuing enemies and doing them harm, for sending messengers. Favours journeys southwards.

Good for buying slaves, who will be strong, loyal, and good, for building, which will be solid and durable, and for voyages, though there will be delays.

Marriage will only last for a while. Bad for marriage, for sowing, for merchandise, for buying livestock. Bad for partnerships, which will end badly and harmfully, and a slave will escape.

26th Lunar Mansion: Pegasus's Shoulder, The Fore-spout of the Water-bucket, The First Spout, The First Drawing, Draining.

Position: This Mansion starts from 21 AQUARIUS 25' 40" and ends at 04 PISCES 17' 09".

Dates: 25th February to 9th March (Ancient), 13th March to 28th March (Current).

Ruling Constellation: The constellation originally associated with this mansion is **Pegasus**. The principal stars associated with this mansion are Scheat (beta Pegasus) and Markab (alpha Pegasus). The current constellation is **Pisces/Aries**.

Nature: Uranus and Jupiter.

Attribute: The Jinn.

Divine Attribute: The Subtle.

Significance: Helps union, love of men, health of captives, destroys prisons and buildings.

Good for making a journey in the first third of the day, but the rest is good for neither journeys nor any other beginning.

Good for building, which will be solid and durable, for buying a slave, who will be loyal and good, for entering a ship, though there will be delays.

Bad for partnerships. Marriage will not last. If captured, he will be in prison for a long time.

27th Lunar Mansion: Pegasus's Wing, The Second Spout, The Lower-spout of the Water-bucket, The Second Drawing, Draining.

Position: This Mansion starts from 04 PISCES 17' 09" and ends at 17 PISCES 08' 34".

Dates: 10th March to 22nd March (Ancient), 29th March to 19th April (Current).

Ruling Constellation: The constellations originally associated with this mansion are **Pegasus and Andromeda**. The principal stars associated with this mansion are Algenib (gamma Pegasus) and Alpheratz (alpha Andromeda). The current constellation is **Aries/Taurus**.

Planets: Neptune and Venus.

Attribute: Humanity.

Divine Attribute: The Uniter.

Significance: Increases harvests, revenues, money, heals illnesses, weakens buildings, prolongs imprisonment, endangers sailors, and helps bringing evils against anyone.

Good for sowing, and useful for trading. Good for marriage.
Indifferent for journeys, except for middle third of night when very bad.

Bad for entrusting something to someone, or lending anything. If starting a partnership, it will begin well but end in harm and conflict. Entering a ship will bring damage, dangers, and travails. A slave bought will be bad.
If captured, he will not leave prison.

28th Lunar Mansion: Fish's Belly, The Belly of the Fish, The Fishes, Pisces.

Position: This Mansion starts from 17 PISCES 08' 34" and ends at 00 ARIES 00' 00".

Dates: 23rd March to 4th April (Ancient), 20th April to 22nd April (Current).

Ruling Constellation: The constellation originally associated with this mansion is **Andromeda**. The principal star associated with this mansion is Mirach (beta Andromeda). The current constellation is **Taurus**.

Planets: Venus and Saturn.

Attribute: The Hierarchy of the Degrees of Existence, not their manifestation.

Divine Attribute: The One Who Elevates by Degrees.

Significance: Increases harvests and commerce, helps the safety of travellers in dangerous places, causes marital harmony, but strengthens prisons and causes loss of treasures.

Good for trade, sowing and medicines. Good for marriage. Indifferent for journeys, except for middle third of night when bad.

Bad for entrusting something to someone, or lending anything. A partnership started will begin well but end badly. A slave bought will be bad, and very proud. If captured, he will not leave prison.

GREGORIAN MANSION DATES
ACCORDING TO WIKIPEDIA

Wikipedia states:
https://en.wikipedia.org/wiki/Lunar_station

"In the traditional Arabic astrological system, the new moon was seen to move through 28 distinct *manāzil* (singular: *manzil* "house") during the normal solar year, each *manzil* lasting, therefore, for about 13 days.

One or more *manazil* were then grouped into a *nawaa* (plural *anwaa*) which were tied to a given weather pattern. In other words, the yearly pattern was divided in the following manner: A year was divided into *anwaa*, each of which was made up of one more *manazil*, which were associated with a dominant star or constellation. These stars and constellations were sometimes, but not always, connected in some way to constellations in the Zodiac.

Moreover, as the *anwaa* repeat on a regular, solar cycle, they can be correlated to fixed points on the Gregorian calendar.

The following table is a breakdown of the *anwaa* and their position on the Gregorian calendar."

Manzil	Associated Nawaa	Significant Stars/Constellations	Zodiac Constellations	Begins on
Sharatān	Al Thurayyā	Sheratan in Aries	--	17 May
Pleione	Al Thurayyā	Pleione in the Pleiades	--	31 May
Al-Butayn	Al Thurayyā	Albatain in the Pleiades	--	13 June
Al-Tuwaibe'	Al Tuwaibe'	Aldebaran	--	26 June
Al-Haq'ah	Al Jawzaa/Gemini	Haq'ah in Orion	Gemini	9 July
Al-Han'ah	Al Jawzaa/Gemini	Alhena in Gemini	Gemini	22 July
Murzim	Murzim	Canis Major	--	4 August
An Nathra	Kulaibain	An Nathra	--	17 August
Alterf	Suhail	Alterf in Leo	Leo	30 August
Dschuba	Suhail	Dschuba	Scorpio	12 September
Azzubra	Suhail			25 September
Assarfa	Suhail			8 October
Auva	Al Wasm	Auva	Virgo	21 October
Simak	Al Wasm	Spica	--	3 November
Syrma	Al Wasm		--	16 November
Az Zubana	Al Wasm	Acuben	Cancer	29 November
Akleel "The Crown"	Murabaania	Corona Borealis	--	12 December
Qalb al Akraab	Murabaania	Antares	Scorpio	25 December
Shaula	Murabaania	Shaula	Scorpio	3 January
Al Naam	Ash Shabt	Ascella and Nunki	Sagittarius	16 January
Al Baldaah	Ash Shabt	Pi Saggitari	Sagittarius	29 January
Saad Al Thabib	The Three Saads	Beta Capricorni	Capricornus	11 February
Saad Balaa	The Three Saads	Saad Balaa	--	26 February
Saad Al Saud	The Three Saads	Saadalsud	Aquarius	11 March
Saad Al Akhbia	Hameemain	Sadachbia	--	24 March
Almuqaddam	Hameemain	Almuqaddam	--	6 April
Al Muakhar	Al Tharaeen	Pollux	Gemini and Aquarius (in the Arab system)	19 April
Alrescha	Al Tharaeen	Alrescha	Gemini and Aquarius (in the Arab system)	2 May

KIRCHER'S COPTIC MANSIONS

THE COPTIC MANSIONS OF THE MOON ACCORDING TO KIRCHER

	George Yeats's Notes see *The Making of Yeats's Vision* II, 419		*De Aegyptiacis Stellarum apellationibus* from *Lingua Aegyptiaca Restituta*, 560-67	*Concerning the Egyptian names of the stars*
	28 Mansions of ☽ 560. Athanasius Kircher	from to	Coptic name Latin translation and comments	transcription and translation
1	♓	0 Aries - 12° 24' Aries	ⲕ︤ⲩⲧⲱⲛ︥ : *piscis* Venter Cæti, sive piscis	[kutôn] *fish the belly of the whale, or the fish*
2	♈ (see Abenragel)	12° 24' Aries - 25 Aries	ⲡⲓⲕⲩⲧⲱⲣⲓⲟⲛ : Piscis Hori caput Arietis authority: Abenragel	[*pi-kutôrion] *fish of Horus the head of Aries / the ram*
3	from 5th degree of ♈ to 9th ♉ The mansions of this joining together	25 Aries - 9 Taurus	ⲕⲟⲗⲓⲱⲛ : statio connectens triangulum prope ventrem cæti	[kolion] *connecting / joining station a triangle near the whale's belly*
4	♉ The Mansion of Hours (also the Hen of the skies with her sons) joining ♉ to 21	9 Taurus - 21 Taurus	ⲱⲣⲓⲁⲥ : statio Hori Gallina cæli, cum filiabus suis (the Pleiades)	[ôrias] *station of Horus the hen of the skies with her daughters (also chicks)*
5	from 21 ♉ to 4 ♊. The eye of ♉	21 Taurus - 4 Gemini	ⲡⲓⲱⲣⲓⲟⲛ : Statio Hori maior oculus ♉	[*pi-ôrion] *greater station of Horus the eye of Taurus / the bull*
6	The Head of ♊. 4 ♊ to 17 ♊ (The Gate)	4 Gemini - 17 Gemini	ⲕⲁⲩⲥⲟⲥ : Claustrum caput ♊	[klusos] *barrier / gate the head of Gemini*
7	17 of ♊ to 30 ♊ (The shoulder blade of the Twin)	17 Gemini - 30 Gemini	ⲕⲗⲁⲣⲓⲁ : (no Latin, Arabic, *Alheuak*) scapulas Geminorum	[klaria] *Gemini's / the Twins' shoulder blades*
8	(The bed of the Lion) 1 of ♋ to 13	0 Cancer - 13 Cancer	ⲡⲓⲙⲁϩⲓ : cubitus (Nili) cubitus Leonis ('lion' is incorrect)	[*pi-mahi] *cubit of the Nile (Nilometer) forepaw of Leo / the lion*
9	(The descent) 13 of ♋ to 21 ♋	13 Cancer - †21 Cancer	ⲧⲉⲣⲙⲉⲗⲓⲁ : statio discensus seu influentiae	[termelia] *station of descent or influence / influx*
10	(The parturition of self) from 21 ♋ 9 ♌	†21 Cancer - †9 Leo	ⲡⲓⲁⲩⲧⲟⲥ : Scipsam parturiens	[*pi-autos] *giving birth to itself*
11	(The Tree in leaf) 9 ♌ 21 ♌	9 Leo - 21 Leo	ϯⲧⲉϩⲛⲓ : Frons frons Leonis	[*ti-tehni] *forehead / brow of Leo / the lion*
12	21 ♌ 4 ♍	21 Leo - 4 Virgo	ⲡⲓⲱⲣⲓⲟⲛ : (no Latin; Greek ᵒⲣᴀⲣᴇⲅⴹ)	[*pi-chômon]
13	(Mansion of love 4 ♍ to 18 ♍)	†0 Virgo - 18 Virgo	ⲁⲥⲫⲩⲗⲓⲁ : statio Amoris	[asphulia] *station of Love*
14	(Mansion of acclamation) 18 ♍ 30 ♍ Latrantius?	18 Virgo - 30 Virgo	ⲁⲃⲩⲕⲓⲁ : statio latrantis forsan à Canicula	[abukia] *station of the barker / dog perhaps from the Dog Star (Sirius)*
15	(Mansion of Highth & depth) 0 ♎ to 13 ♎	0 Libra - 13 Libra	ⲭⲱⲣⲓⲧⲟⲥ : statio altitudinis	[choritos] *station of height and / or depth*
16	(Mansion of propitiation) 13 ♎ 26 ♎	13 Libra - 26 Libra	ⲭⲁⲙⲃⲁⲗⲓⲁ : statio propiliationis	[chambalia] *station of propitiation*
17	26 ♎ 1 ♏	26 Libra - 11 Scorpio	ⲡⲣⲓⲧⲓⲟⲓ : (no Latin, even Arabic not transliterated)	[pritihi] *(describes the name of Aquarius)*
18	(The crown) 1 ♏ 21 ♏	9 Scorpio - 21 Scorpio	ⲥⲧⲉⲫⲁⲛⲓ : Corona	[stephani] *the crown*
19	(The Heart of Scorpio) 21 ♏ 4 ♐	21 Scorpio - 4 Sagittarius	ⲕⲁⲣⲟⲓⲁⲛ : Cor cor Scorpii	[karthian] *the heart the heart of Scorpio*
20	(Mansion of chastity) 4 ♐ 17 ♐	4 Sagittarius - 17 Sagittarius	ⲁⲅⲅⲓⲁ : Sancta	[aggia / angia] *saved, inviolable, chaste*
21	(Mansion of delight & favour (influence)) 17 ♐ 30 ♐	17 Sagittarius - 30 Sagittarius	ⲛⲓⲙⲁⲙⲣⲉϩ : statio gratiae, & iucunditatis	[*ni-mamreh] *station of favour and delight*
22	The State. 6 ♑ to 12 ♑	0 Capricorn - 13 Capricorn	ⲡⲟⲗⲓⲥ : Civitas	[polis] *the city-state*
23	(The sacrifice of arm) 12 ♑ 25 ♑	13 Capricorn - 25 Capricorn	ⲩⲡⲉⲩⲧⲱⲥ : Brachium sacrificii	[upeutôs] *the arm of sacrifice*
24	(The absorption of arm—Beatitude) 25 ♑ to 9 ♒	†29 Capricorn - 9 Aquarius	ⲩⲡⲉⲩⲣⲓⲧⲱⲥ : Beatitudo, sive brachium absorptum	[upeuritôs] *beatitude / felicity, or the arm swallowed*
25	(The beatitude of beatitudes) 9 ♒ to 21 ♒	9 Aquarius - 21 Aquarius	ⲩⲡⲉⲩⲛⲉⲩⲧⲏⲥ : Beatitudo beatitudinum, sive Brachium brachiorum	[upeuneutès] *felicity of felicities, or the arm of arms*
26	(The concealed arm) 21 ♒ 4 ♓	21 Aquarius - 4 Pisces	ⲩⲡⲉⲩⲟⲉⲣⲓⲁⲛ : Brachium absconditum	[upeutherian] *the concealed arm*
27	(Mansion of the first budding) 4 ♓ to 17 ♓	4 Pisces - 17 Pisces	ⲁⲣⲧⲩⲗⲟⲥ : Statio prioris germinationis	[artulos] *station of the first budding / germination*
28	(The final generation) 17 ♓ to 30 –	17 Pisces - 30 Pisces	ⲁⲣⲧⲩⲗⲟⲥⲓⲁ : Posterior germinatio	[artulosia] *later budding / germination*

* In Coptic Egyptian, the definite article is ⲡⲓ 'pi' for the masculine, ϯ 'ti' for the feminine and ⲛⲓ 'ni' for the common plural.

† Anomalous degree values — the misprints were corrected in *Oedipus Aegyptiacus*, although that also has its own mistakes.

BIBLIOGRAPHY

Thank you to the following Authors:

1.   Athanasius Kircher.
2.   Haly Abenragel.
3.   William Butler Yeats.

Thank you to the following websites:

1.   https://en.wikipedia.org/wiki/Lunar_station

Printed in Great Britain
by Amazon

47932577R00024